# A DOSE OF MOTIVATION

Thanks for
the support!

*W. B. Smith*

# A DOSE OF MOTIVATION

*Taking ownership of your life, tapping into your potential, and stepping into your purpose.*

Warren B. Wright, M.Ed., LPC-Intern, NCC

A DOSE OF MOTIVATION

Copyright © 2019 by Warren Wright

Editor: Adam Clay Webb
Author photo: TreVoy Kelly
Cover design: Eddison Smith III

This book is not intended to serve as a model of medical and/or mental health treatment. Consult with a primary care practitioner or mental health provider as needed for any severe concerns. The intent of the author is to provide guidance, inspiration, empowerment, and growth.

This book is dedicated to

My Grandma Martha and Aunt Pat; two of my earthly

anchors who have now become my spiritual anchors.

May you both rest in peace.

# Contents

# **<u>Introduction</u>**

We live in a medicated society, one in which whenever we experience discomfort or hurt, we seek out some magic pill to numb the pain. Today, people are unwilling to sit in discomfort. Their tolerance for pain has waned to almost nothing. Painkillers, shame and doubt, have come to define our society. The world has become a convenient express environment where we assess our self-worth on the number of followers we have on social media or the number of achievements we possess. We have become so socialized to repress our emotions, that we don't even know how to identify the way we feel. We have lost touch with our true selves, with our own emotions, and identities. We are either chastised or shamed for showing any signs of vulnerability. Whether explicitly or implicitly, we are taught that we cannot show signs of "weakness", and that we MUST feel happy. This has caused a major shift in the human experience.

Life is a journey, one in which we get to experience. A journey full of love, pain, and curiosity. Living life sometimes comes with its hardships, and other times comes with its victories. The way in which we decide on how it affects us personally begins with a choice that each individual must make.

Today, decide on how you want to live your life. Make a commitment to be uniquely you. Find meaning and value in every situation life throws at you, and always remember it is okay to not be okay at times.

This book is for those like me who sit, think, ponder, and reflect. It is also for those who are trying to find meaning to life and dream BIG. It is for those who experience periods of self-doubt, and for those who need a little inspiration. Each chapter opens with a quote and ends with a reflection question (RQ) for you to take the time to think about. You are invited to jot down your thoughts, and even share them with others. Each of these quotes were created because of some hardship I had to endure, or some lesson I learned from my life experiences. These quotes have helped me to motivate myself; For this reason, I would like to share them and this book with you. In each chapter, I pray that you find some hope. My desire is for this book to evoke a sense of change, ambition, and courage. Whether you read a chapter a day or read it all in one sitting, I hope it serves you well. Thank you for taking the time to read this book and may the words in it be your dose of motivation.

# <u>Chapter 1</u>

## The Power of Words

*"Your words have power. Use them wisely."*

Words—like the ones on this page—are used to form meaning. They are intentionally constructed to form sentences, to relay information, and more critically, achieve communication. Words are a part of the everyday human language. In every culture, within each household, and among friends, words are used to share messages of love, hope, and togetherness. I believe that life and death are in the power of the tongue[1], meaning that the words we form in our mouth can either lift someone up or tear them down. What we speak over our own lives can just as well have the same effect on us.

---

[1] Proverbs 18:21 (KJV)

Saying "I am dumb," "I am ugly," or "I will always be broke" is speaking negativity into your life. Eventually, you will begin to believe these self-defeating messages, which will in turn impede on your personal growth. We do this unintentionally and mistakenly to ourselves all the time. If you have failed an exam as a college student you may have said something like, "I will never graduate," "I am the dumbest in my class," "I am a failure," or the universal phrase, "I'm not good enough." Often times we misinterpret what we do with who we are. We get the notion that our mistakes and shortcomings are a reflection of our identity. Other times we allow others to define us by our mistakes. Yes, I said *allow*. Sometimes those critics are our own family members and close friends. Don't get me wrong, we all have haters and naysayers that try to hinder us from growing just because we have something they don't. However, people learn how to treat us based on how we treat ourselves. The things they say to us are usually but a reflection of the things we say to and about ourselves. How they treat us is usually closely knit to how we treat ourselves.

What we have to understand is that what we have done or will possibly do in the future does not define who we are. We may not be able to control our circumstances or avoid all mistakes, but we can certainly control how we react to such. Instead of placing labels on ourselves such as *inadequate, failure,* or *loser,* we should embrace our imperfections. By embracing your imperfections, you are essentially accepting yourself wholeheartedly. You are saying that in spite of all my mistakes, my downfalls, and failed chances, I choose to be me. I unapologetically choose to be me. In this you become authentic. You become an advocate in your own life to live up to bigger and better things. You begin to say that "I am amazing in spite of my mistakes" and "I am somebody even if they don't like me."

The power of *I am* is one of the greatest statements we all could use. What comes after that *I am* is what changes our mindset about ourselves and what we can accomplish. "I am great," "I am loved," and "I am currently without extra financial stability and that it okay" all have different meanings than "I suck," "I am hated," and "I am broke." Yeah, I know it is easier said than done, but I'll betcha, if you change the way you view yourself by starting with "I am" statements, your self-confidence, efficacy, and motivation to imagine yourself higher will increase. That is when you will be able to walk in your truth and own it. You will be able to stand alone and muster the courage to carry on. With *I am* statements, your quality of life will shift in a positive direction, giving way to new manifestations of greatness in your life. Your *I am* statements will become so profound that you will be able to declare them doubtlessly.

Today, substitute those self-defeating thoughts with statements of self-motivation. Empower yourself today with "I am" statements so you can serve as an example for someone else tomorrow. Always love yourself. Our words have the power to manifest either greatness or defeat into our lives; we must decide what we speak into being. Be intentional with the words you direct at others, and even more so with words directed towards yourself. Your words truly have power. I pray you use them to uplift yourself and others. Repeat the following phrase: "What I say I am is who I will eventually become." I wonder how repeating those words will change your outlook on life.

## RQs

What comes up for you after repeating the phrase above? How does it resonate with you mentally, emotionally, or spiritually?

# Notes

# **<u>Chapter 2</u>**

## Accept Yourself

*"You are enough!"*

Before writing this chapter, I took a breath—a very deep and deliberate breath. That breath was for those who died without accepting who they really were, and for those who are still struggling to accept themselves even today. Accepting yourself fully is not an event, but rather a process. It takes time. In my opinion, self-reflection is a key component of self-acceptance. Self-reflection is a practice which brings about awareness, insight, and meaning to one's life. Accepting yourself fully is an action taken in order to own your imperfections, mistakes, gifts, and talents—all of you. I believe a core factor that hinders people from accepting themselves is this false belief of not being worthy, the feeling of not being enough. My friend, you are just enough.

We shy away from confidence to avoid appearing arrogant. We belittle ourselves with the expectation to look less than because we don't want any unwanted attention (as we don't feel deserving of it). With this mindset, we are not fully presenting ourselves to the world. We go through life presenting ourselves through the lens of our parents' opinions or friends' expectations of us. We must instead put ourselves first. We too often become the last task on our to-do lists, taking no time to be the top priority in our own lives.

Not being able to accept yourself or another person stifles connection, and we human beings live for and through connection. When we are not able to accept ourselves and aren't authentic with our relatives, peers, and friends, we are unable to fully connect with those around us. We live in a world where human connection is critical, and acceptance is a major component to human connection. Without accepting ourselves first, we are unable to teach others how to accept us. My friend, you matter. What you experience, how you feel, every fiber in your being—it all matters. Accept yourself. Accept that limp in your step. Accept that pimple on your chin. Accept that stutter in your speech. Accept *you*!

At birth, I was given the name Warren Brandon Wright. Growing up, I was always called Brandon. In my family, many people used their middle names (for some reason that even to date has eluded me). Up until about the fifth grade, I was called Brandon by my teachers and classmates. In fifth grade is where I became known as Warren. If I remember correctly, it was because there was another Brandon in my class, and I did not like it one bit. "Warren? Why would my parents name me that?". "I didn't look like a Warren". "What does that name even mean?" These thoughts cycled through my head. Looking back, I guess that was my first identity crisis (laughs to self).

For some time after I became known as Warren, I didn't like it. It didn't fit me. I didn't like my name. Some people would say "that's crazy", or ask jeeringly, "why don't you like your name?". And my answer was always the same: I didn't feel worthy of that name. In my head, Warren was an older, white man's name. I was neither of the two. It's crazy now that I'm older and love my name, but back when I was younger, that was my experience. Warren was a name in I believed belonged to someone who was powerful, influential, and worthy. I saw myself as none of those. As a child, I was often timid, soft-spoken, and didn't feel enough. I remember trying to present myself a certain way to fit in. I remember not feeling heard, feeling like I didn't truly belong anywhere. Just like me, many others go through life feeling lost, struggling to ask for help.

Everyone wants to belong somewhere or with a certain crowd. Everyone has their bouts of feeling lonely and afraid of people's reactions and opinions. The thing about feeling lonely and afraid is that it's not openly accepted. Our parents and friends will tell us to "suck it up", "keep moving", or "don't be a punk." Showing signs or sharing experiences of uncomfortable feelings with people who lack *emotional intelligence* will only foster isolation and further damage.

Now that I am older, more mature, and engage in self-reflection, I am aware that I had to grow into my name. I am aware that it had to have taken time. Warren is a name passed down from generations of men who were hard workers, dedicated to taking care of their families, and who displayed drive. Both my granddad and dad are named Warren. When I look into their lives and learn about their past, I am grateful for the name Warren. I am grateful that my granddad was present in my dad's life, and I am grateful that my dad was present in my life. I hope to exude the drive, confidence, and character of them both to my future generations of sons. Through conversations and interactions with both of them, I see motivation, strength, and what it means to be a man of faith. I am able to see myself in them because I am a representation of them. Now when I look in the mirror and see my reflection, I can smile. I can smile because I am now Warren who is powerful, influential, and worthy. My expectation of what my name stood for is what I have grown into, it is what I had to believe for myself. I accepted my name. I am still on the journey of accepting myself.

Sharing my personal story of accepting my name with a mentee fostered a conversation of vulnerability and connection. My mentee, shocked that I used to dislike my name, was opened to share his own personal experience of accepting himself. He shared with me his personal struggle of accepting his voice. He shared that it is still a struggle but, that talking with me gave him insight on acceptance. Growing up, he was bullied in school for not having a deep voice or what he believed to be a "manly" voice. Classmates and peers at school would tease and bully him by telling him he "sounded like a girl." This pushed him to feeling ashamed of his voice. He further explained that sometimes when he talks with people, he will intentionally deepen the tone of his voice to sound more "manly." Shocked and a little amazed, I told him that I never realized that his voice sounded "off", or that he would lower the tone of his voice to sound "manly." He didn't like his voice. My mentee was ridiculed and shamed for his voice, something over which he had no control. That shame and criticism from others impeded on his personal growth and still serves as a barrier for accepting himself. Until he is able to accept his voice, he will not be able to wholly accept himself.

We were able to laugh about each other's story because through sharing about accepting or working on accepting ourselves we formed a stronger connection. We live in a world where humans crave connection and acceptance. Without accepting ourselves first, how are we able to teach others how to accept us?

By accepting ourselves, we are able to stand in courage and exude authenticity. We are able to accept that even when we show people who we are honestly, we will be okay if they still choose not to accept us.

Today, remind yourself that you are enough. Accept your human flaws and imperfections. Engage in some self-reflection and remember to show up in life honestly. Take a breath. Inhale acceptance and exhale the negative beliefs about yourself.

## RQs

What are some things you still need to accept about yourself? How will you know that you have accepted yourself fully?

# Notes

# **Chapter 3**

## Isolation

*"In isolation lies inner strength."*

In our darkest hours, we are flooded with despair, grief, and loneliness. It is in those dark times that our lights are awakened in order to create a path to a brighter future. Life shows us that sometimes we are stuck in a complacent state of mind and need to sit in isolation in order to elevate ourselves. This is lonesome, but a necessary process of *introspection*. Sometimes that elevation could be a big career change or a move to a different part of the world away from our friends and loved ones. When you are in a period of utter defeat, or in some desolate wasteland of life where there is no one within arm's reach, dig deep and find your inner strength. It is in those times where your strength from within will surface, and you will beget the heart of the lion.

This introspection brought forth from isolation is what prepares us for our next move in life. A lot of times we yearn for more in life, or we are so bogged down by life's struggles that we can't see our way out. Things become cloudy, and we lose the sight of our purpose in life. We lose the vision given to us. It is in those times where your back may be against the wall or you have to remove yourself from distractions in order to reach deep within yourself to pull out greatness. With that greatness, you will be able to elevate yourself in life. Elevate yourself!

For me, when I reach a plateau of stagnation or hopelessness, I remove myself from everything—family, friends, etc. I go into this period of self-discovery. I pray, meditate, and write. I like to call this *voluntary isolation*. I do this in order to envision my next step in life. It is a way of embracing myself for a new chapter. I do this to understand what I'm not fully grasping in order to have a fuller life. You see, life sometimes throws distractions at you or put things in your way so you will not live out your purpose. In those times, it's best to remove the cloudiness. Removing the clutter helps you see things clearer. This voluntary isolation helps you to become more attuned with a higher power; I consider that higher power to be God. It is then when I am stimulated to make a bigger move in life.

For example, in order to secure a legit future after graduation, I had to separate myself from the partying, going out with friends, and other unnecessary activities. I knew that I had to manage my time more wisely. I had to focus on things that would keep me on the path to achieving my goals. In that, I isolated myself not for the worse, but for the better. In this self-isolation, I dug deep and found the strength to apply to graduate programs, revise my resume, and excel in my interviews. The noise in my head had been silenced, and the light in my eyes were brightened. Now as I sit and write this chapter, I smile, because with that period of isolation, I am now finishing up my last semester in my graduate program while progressing through another form of isolation in order to complete this book. It's funny how things work out sometimes.

While my form of isolation may be voluntary, others may be involuntary. Someone may have taken the last few punches that life has thrown at them. They may feel lost, as if life has taken everything from them. My friend, if you feel that way, please know that you have the strength to carry on just another day. You have all the needed resources in you to step into your purpose and live out your dreams. In isolation is where you find your inner strength.

We strive to have better things in life and desire to have more. When I say more, do not think materialistically.

15

Now don't get me wrong, it's great to have nice things. When elevating in life, material things may come, but this is the icing on the cake, and not the cake itself.

What people want and hope for is to have more in life, more gratification and more satisfaction. We want to make a difference. We want to have a brighter future, even if it means taking risks. Where we go wrong in maintaining motivation and a plan of action is that we have these unrealistic expectations. Such expectations hinder us from taking that leap of faith. We believe that things should go smoothly and without hiccups, but such is hardly the reality. We become stuck on what it should look like instead of seizing the moment and embracing the change. We are wired to do what helps us feel safe and comfortable. In our comfort, we lose our chances to step into our potential and to step into a fuller, more elevated chapter in life. Dare to live. Live out your dreams. It's time to fully take control of your life and live a greater and fuller life, even though it may not look how you planned it or expected it to be. Learn to live in order to elevate in life.

There are several times when those failed expectations on how you plan to elevate your life come with these twin concepts: doubt and fear. Doubt is that small, nagging voice of uncertainty when we are about to make a decision. It is that "what if" brat that we can't get rid of. Fear is that second voice that creeps in and ruins the moment when you decide to do something bigger and bolder in life. Fear, doubt's twin, is the emotional experience of something that is an unreal threat or response to a decision. Fear is the intense reaction of inadequacy or anxiety we feel when doubt says, "they won't like your idea," "he will never date you," or "you're not enough." These annoying twins wreak havoc in our lives by constantly reminding us of our imperfections, limitations, and false beliefs that we will be in harm's way if we decide to live a courageous life. Doubt and fear push you into a deep sense of isolation.

You see, in the beginning, doubt and fear are having a good time creating chaos in your life. They don't believe that anything will stop them. They are both reinforced by people in your circle that say, "don't go back to school," "why are you wasting your time on that dream," or "you won't be able to start that business." These are only some examples people have heard or experienced mentally for themselves. I'm sure you can come up with other doubtful and fear-ridden messages. To me, doubt and fear are fucking annoying! Yeah, I said it. Excuse my language, friend. They are like those family members you really can't stand to be around for the holidays, or that one coworker who is always running their mouth about nonsense.

My friend, I gotta be real with you and say, I still continue to be bothered by doubt and fear to this very day. Doubt and fear have always put me through a struggle.

There are three phases that I have to go through in order to work through both doubt and fear which will be discussed more fully in the next chapter—awareness, acknowledgment, and acceptance.

## RQs

When did you experience a period of isolation? What was it like for you? What did you learn about yourself?

# Notes

# <u>Chapter 4</u>

## Overcoming Doubt and Fear

*"Doubt and fear are thieves set in place to stop the becoming of your vision."*

Doubt, whether from within the mind or some external source, is a destroyer. It is created in order to creep in and steal the enjoyment and excitement from your life. Doubt is, by all means, a nuisance when it comes to young entrepreneurs starting their businesses. It is the very thing along with fear, that keeps a senior in high school from moving away from home. It also impedes the personal growth of professionals who want to advance in their field of study and are too hesitant, because they are convinced that the next move in life will not be as satisfying or will push them out of their comfort zones. Doubt is the thief set in place to stop the becoming of your vision.

I am currently on this wave of being authentic and showing up honestly to the best of my ability. In order to help you and other readers do the same, I want to share with you my own battle with doubt and fear while writing this book. In the process of writing the previous chapter, I was hit with several doubtful thoughts about this project. Honestly, I was going to stop writing and let those thoughts win. I was seriously ready to accept defeat. While processing the thoughts and engaging in *self-reflection*, I had to literally work through them. While working through them, I came up with three steps, and was finally at the right place of accepting a new thought or idea about my writing. As you can see, those doubtful thoughts did not defeat me.

While penning and processing these thoughts, I came up with the following in order to overcome them: awareness, acknowledgment, and acceptance. For me, I had to become *aware* of their structure and origin. I had to *acknowledge* that they were there. Also, I had to *accept* that I had power over them in order to overcome them. You see, those thoughts that were fueled by doubt were trying to stop me from becoming a writer, or at least use my words to inspire others. They were a distraction in order to take my mind off of this project, but I said, "not so." Let's look into these three phases of overcoming fear and doubt.

## Awareness

Being aware of doubt and fear is the initial step in overcoming these two evil twins. Awareness is knowing what triggers your doubt or fear and being conscious of what they are telling you. For me, it was "what if people don't like your book?", "what if you send this off to an editor or publisher and they take the credit for it?", and "what if you fail as a writer?" Having thoughts like this in our head feeds us with solid discouragement, and we all get them from time to time. What I would suggest you do is to write them down. Whether you have to write them down on a sheet of paper, in a diary, or on the mirror like I did, write them down. Look them over, study them, and visualize them as a projection from outside of your mind.

While writing the previous chapter, I was struck so hard by doubt and fear. In order to get through them, I literally took a break from writing/typing because at the moment, doubt and fear had crept up and whispered the ultimate phrase: "you're not enough." It is that same phrase that I use as motivation to better myself and become *more* each day. I pondered, "How can I write a book about shifting one's mindset from not being enough to being enough and I can't even get over my own doubt and fear?" I had to dig deep and bring out some new skills I taught myself in order to be aware of my personal doubt and fear.

In the awareness phase, you have to dig deep and write down what doubt, and fear are telling you. You have to write it down and really flip it inside out. The awareness phase helps you to be proactive rather than reactive. It helps you prepare for when they arise in order for you to eventually take control. Having a pen and paper by hand will be your best friend. In my case, having a full body mirror and Expo markers worked just fine.

**Acknowledgment**

By acknowledging your doubtful thoughts and fear, you will be able to label and identify them, and externalize the thought from your own identity. For me, I named my thoughts as "fear," "anxiety," and "insecurity." I had to remind myself that my thoughts are not who I am but are what I experience. Doubt and fear will always be around, and I will use them as a stepping stool in order to live out my dreams and purpose in life. In this second phase, understand that fear and doubt will be natural conditions you may experience in life. What you have to understand is that they will never get the best of you or control you if you don't let them. What I had to remind myself is that doubt, and fear will always be present, but I cannot and WILL NOT let them get the best of me.

## Acceptance

In the acceptance phase, you have the capacity to rewrite or retrain your mind to choose another thought. This is where you regain control in efforts of adopting a new ideal and way of viewing yourself. Whether it's a thought to motivate your career as a singer, DJ, or graduate student, adopt a new thought about yourself. When you have doubt, always remember to lean into hope. Hope gives you strength in moments where you feel weak. Hope helps you smile when you are in pits of despair. Hope gives you courage when you feel defeated.

I was once hired to be a speaker for a health department diversity training. This training program wanted to incorporate mental health speakers. While presenting at a national conference, my topic piqued the interests of two women in my conference session. They came and talked with me after my presentation and told me that they were looking for speakers for their upcoming training program, and that I was the speaker they were looking for. Long story short, I accepted their offer. I was especially excited about this, as it was my first speaking gig.

While presenting on labels, I shared with the attendees that it was my first time presenting at a conference, and that while in the process of creating my presentation, I labeled myself as a "rookie." As you know, once I spoke those words out loud to myself, other thoughts came racing to mind fueled by those two evil gremlins doubt and fear. I labeled myself as a rookie because while practicing, I continued to stumble over my words, misspelled words in my presentation, and felt insecure. The label rookie disempowered me to the point where I thought about playing sick the day of the presentation to avoid feeling not enough, not educated enough, and as a rookie.

What I had to do was revert to the three steps of overcoming doubt and fear in order to gain my power back. I was aware that this was my first conference presentation and that it was coming up shortly. I acknowledged that I felt "fearful," "nervous," and "anxious." I accepted that it was my first conference presentation, and everything will not be perfect. I also accepted that the more I gave conference presentations, the better I would become as a speaker. I took the time to sit in vulnerability and mustered up the courage to share my story. With that, I was brave and authentic in sharing my experiences with doubt and fear. If I would have played sick, I would not have been hired as a speaker that same day after my presentation. They paid me $1,370.50 by the way, and that number I will never forget.

What I've noticed is that it's time to live brave, dream big, and be fearless. By embracing bravery, thinking or dreaming higher, and living fearlessly you're simply being B.O.L.D.! You are taking the chance on being **b**rave, **o**ptimistic, **l**eading with your heart, and having a **d**eserving approach on life. When you make up in your mind to be fearless and dare to live, you are being transformed to a higher way of thinking eventually leading to a higher way of living. You are taking back ownership of your life and embarking on a journey towards your destiny. You are saying yes to life's adventures and saying I'll be okay if I run into some unexpected trials and barriers. Nothing should stand in the way of the becoming of your vision. Expect greatness and accept nothing less my friend.

## RQs

What has doubt and fear kept you away from? What are they telling you now? Give it a name. What new idea will you adapt to overcome doubt and fear?

# Notes

# **<u>Chapter 5</u>**

## The Art of Pain

*"Pain pushes you into your purpose."*

On July 17, 2016, I lost an anchor in my life. That anchor was a loving, sassy, warm-hearted woman. That anchor was my grandma. When I got the news of her passing, it was something I just couldn't accept, a reality I could not face. I guess I was in denial. I'll never forget the moment I broke down and began to weep. It was a salient moment that I'll never forget. The day after she passed my family and I ate at a local diner in our hometown. While eating, my parents continued to ask me if I was okay and I would respond, "yeah I'm okay," or "I'm fine." My grandma and I were very close, so I assumed that because I wasn't showing any emotions, my parents and younger brother were worried about me. After we ate, we were leaving out of the diner and I can just remember walking behind everyone. There was something about the sun; it somehow reminded me of my grandma. And the tears came streaming down my face. I was paralyzed. This was my moment to finally weep and grieve the loss of my grandma. I was overwhelmed with emotions, and this was my breaking point. All of the sadness, anger, and pain I felt came rushing to the surface. "She's gone. My grandma is gone."—that is all I can remember saying.

In preparation for my grandma's funeral, there were family members chosen to speak including my older cousin, who sang a very beautiful song. I wanted to do something for my grandma because we were so close but didn't know exactly what to do. I didn't want to just stand up and give a small speech about my grandma. I wanted it to be meaningful, so I wrote a letter to her and presented it at the funeral. While writing the letter I experienced the bitter-sweetness of having had the opportunity to know her, and at the same time now having the emptiness of having to let her go. In the process of writing the letter, I had one of those "aha!" moments. At that moment, I realized God was speaking to me. For some time, more like years, I ignored my calling or purpose on becoming a writer. In that moment of writing my grandma's letter, I realized that I was finally writing, and so I smiled. I don't believe God took my grandma from this earth solely to make me write, yet I do believe that it was a moment of revelation for me. It helped me understand that when you have a purpose on earth and don't fulfill it, it will seek you out. In this case, during a time where I was experiencing pain from the passing of my grandma, I met my purpose to use my words in order to touch and inspire others. Inspire and touch people is exactly what I did during my speech at the funeral service.

Many people came to me afterward and gave words of support and told me I did a great job. My dad's friend was touched by my words because it reminded him of his own relationship with his grandma. Before we left the church to go to the burial site, my great aunt and older sister to my grandma stopped me and said, "Now I don't know, but I think you're meant to be a preacher or a speaker." After sharing that I touched her with my words and that my grandma would have been proud of me I responded, "Thanks, Auntie. I would like to be a speaker someday." This short conversation with her gave me confirmation that my words are influential and that I have a gift.

Like many others, I ignored the call to use my gift. I believed that I didn't have the right tools or knowledge to write. I believe that my life had to be set up a certain way and I had to be in perfect time in order to use my gifts and talents. What I've learned is that God will not give you the tools for your next chapter in life until you are done using the current tools he provided. Once we use those tools and fulfill what's needed in the present chapter and until we are done experiencing the current chapter, he'll give you the next needed materials and supplies for the next chapter in life. Until you tap into your gifts and talents and use what you already have, you'll always be stuck in that "what if" stage in life. We always wonder, hope, and wish for something to happen, or for our lives to take off, but this never happens. We never put in the work to get there, and never invest in ourselves to move forward in life. If you never act on your purpose in life, it will eventually die, and the people you were supposed to influence or motivate will never receive what you were meant to give them. You see our purpose, gifts, and talents are bigger than us. They are not for us, but for others in the world.

When we refuse to act on our purpose in life, it will find us and nag us until we eventually give in and explore it for ourselves. Sometimes your purpose will visit you in thoughts or nudge your mind when you're in the line at the grocery store. Other times your purpose will wake you out of your sleep and nag, "what about me?" For me, it was the latter. Before I get to my purpose waking me up, let's rewind and go back to when I was called to write.

## The Call

During the summer after my sophomore year in college, I went back home to live with my parents. Like other college students who know the struggle, there's nothing to do back home after you've had an amazing year hanging out with friends. Because I stayed on campus during the year, I had to move out of my residence hall for the summer, I had neither classes nor a job for the summer, so I had no reason to stay. Before the school year ended, I changed my major, which was a huge move in my college journey. Being a future-oriented person, I wanted to know what options I had after college with a psychology degree. That summer I prayed and asked God what I was meant to do on earth and where I was supposed to end up in life. This was a constant prayer many nights because I felt lost. Then I had THE dream!

In this dream, I remember lying in bed when a high school teacher of mine entered my room. We were having a short conversation when all of a sudden, her English turned into some strange tongue. I could no longer understand her. Puzzled, I began to tell her, "I can't understand you. What are you saying?" While she continued to talk in this foreign language, a bright light filled my room and through the door came this angel whose wings were magnificent and massive. He walked up behind my former high school teacher and said, "She is saying you're meant to be a writer." And in the blink of an eye they both were gone.

A cold peaceful presence washed over me, and I woke up soaked in tears. This presence I soon realized was not cold and frigid, but it was a cool sense of relief and realization. The presence can be described as joy, peace, or love. It was a breath of fresh air. That was a definite answer to my prayers, so I began to write quotes here and there but did not act on it or explore what it meant to be a writer. Again, I was fearful and doubted my gifts as a writer. I second-guessed myself and my abilities and never fully believed in myself. When you get a definite answer like I did, my friend, don't ignore it. Take it for its worth and explore what you can do with it. It is yours and nobody can take it from you. They may criticize your gifts or talents or not believe in you and that's okay. What's yours is yours and I repeat, no one can take it from you. When you get out of your own head and own way, then you'll be able to fully walk in your purpose and reap the harvest of using your gifts and talents.

**Purpose awakening**

I remember, for one full week, waking up in the middle of the night and finding it impossible to fall asleep again. It was between the same time each night— 3 to 5 am. I thought that it was something in my room disturbing me while sleeping, so I decided to set a timer on my tv to turn it off. No difference. I decided to close my curtains fully to block the light in the stairwell outside of my bedroom window and that didn't help. Around the fifth or sixth night of waking up abruptly, I was frustrated, but I took a breath and asked God, "What do you want?" By this time, I just had this hunch or sense that he was trying to get my attention—it worked. What I realized it to be was my purpose waking me up. I looked over at my closet mirror where I wrote out quotes and small excerpts and began to mentally write the introduction and first chapter of this book in my head. It was as if the words came rushing at me and I couldn't get them out of my head. Eventually, I fell back to sleep and when I woke up, I wrote them out as if there was no time lapse; every word was etched vividly into my mind. Before I started on the introduction and first chapter, the only thing I had for my book was its title. I had little to no inspiration to write for a few weeks after choosing a title. God eventually allowed my purpose to awaken me to get some more work done and so I worked.

That experience taught me that when you have a calling on your life and a purpose destined to fulfill, you cannot outrun it or ignore it. It will eventually catch up with you. Whatever purpose you have to fulfill on this earth my friend, don't ignore it. You will definitely lose sleep like me if you do and feel uneasy because you are not doing the work you're meant to do on this earth.

A Dose of Motivation

## RQs

What painful experience pushed you into your purpose?
When did you experience a purpose awakening?

# Notes

# **Chapter 6**

## Be the Change

*"Imagine how far in life you will be if you stop saying, "I can't."*

"I can't" is such a powerful statement. It's the statement people give power to when they believe that their best isn't good enough and if they feel like their abilities can't match up to their ambitions. It's this small phrase that hinders change. As stated in the first chapter, words have power, and "I can't" has the power to hold us back from taking chances, risks, and embracing change. We have no control over our external environment. We do, however, have control over our internal environment, over our own minds. When we want things to change, we tend to change the things around us instead of looking inward and changing the self first. I believe for change to truly occur, one must turn their perspective inward in order to bring about change outside of the self. You are the catalyst for change in your life. It all starts with you. Change begins with you.

As a counselor, I have had many opportunities to help clients make changes in their lives, whether it be specifically for academics, relationships, or emotional wellness. It is an honor to be a part of someone's journey of self-discovery and change. One common theme I've noticed from sitting with clients in their pain, struggle, and trauma, is that they continued to be in a cycle of unending chaos or confusion because they tried their best to change their environment, never making the decision to change themselves (until they came in for counseling). Once they were aware that they had no control over anything but themselves, they relinquished that control and embraced ownership for their own lives. They made a choice to stop saying "I can't". They started changing their negative thought patterns. They set boundaries in their relationships and learned to love themselves.

A lot like life, change is a process that occurs constantly over time. Sometimes you just have to trust the process. Like the caterpillar's process of becoming a butterfly, you too must go through a transition of uncertainty, vulnerability, and feeling afraid. Don't be stuck in life wishing, hoping, and dreaming. Please don't hold yourself back anymore by saying "I can't". Change starts with the self, and once you're able to embrace change and get out of your own way, maybe you too can break out of your cocoon and fly while others admire your unique abilities and beauty.

## RQs

When in life have the words "I can't" stopped you from moving forward? How were you able to embrace change

# Notes

# <u>Chapter 7</u>

## Risk-Taker

*"Sacrifice today. Successful tomorrow."*

The quote above really speaks volumes. Taking a risk in life can be viewed as a dangerous, yet exciting action. You gamble on what is for what is to come. If the risk turns out to be a smart move, you feel great about your decision. If the risk turns out sour and goes left, you feel disappointed in the outcome, and often scold yourself for having not played it safe. Either way, you should still feel great about taking calculated risks, because you didn't get in your own way and block opportunities. Risk-takers usually go out on a limb hoping that whatever happens turns out okay and is beneficial for them in the long run. Risk-takers usually go against the naysayers and choose not to conform, because they want to live a true and authentic life for themselves. The sacrifices we make today, whether big or small, can lead to successes tomorrow when the rewards of risks are reaped.

Back in my undergraduate years of college, I took a risk of changing my major from pre-nursing to psychology as a sophomore. While in my psychology classes, I found it interesting learning about the human mind and behaviors. My health psychology class piqued my interest in becoming a medical/health psychologist. My aspiration of helping people along with my health science background from high school and course credits from my nursing major influenced me to pursue a minor in public health. The risk of changing my major led me to take up psychology classes where I met one of my professors who informed me about counseling. After having a short conversation with my professor after class, I shared my interest in medical/ health psychology and explained to her what I saw myself doing in the future. She said, "hmm", and asked me if I ever considered pursuing a job in the field of counseling. From that conversation, I researched everything I could about the field of counseling and the requirements to become one. My professor and I had several one-on-one meetings where she shared with me her background in counseling and how she obtained her Ph.D. in Counseling Psychology. From those conversations, that professor planted a seed that would eventually blossom into the career I have today. Taking the risk to change my major allowed me to successfully be accepted into a fantastic counseling program where I received my Master of Education in clinical mental health counseling.

Fast forward two years later while finishing that same counseling program, I accepted an internship position in Savannah, Georgia, where I worked in a college counseling center. For three days out of the week, I would drive to Savannah in order to apply the knowledge I've learned from my classes and practice my counseling skills. Of course, I loved every day of it, because the other counselors were so supportive in my journey on becoming a counselor. The environment allowed growth and development, which were important for me professionally as well as personally. I did carpool with another colleague in my program because we both were accepted as interns there. Driving one hour there in the morning and one hour back in the evening was fun with her, because we became the best of friends and closer as colleagues. For some people, they didn't understand why I put so many miles on my blue 2003 Honda Civic, but for me, it was a sacrifice I had to make in order to get the best training and experience to be a well-rounded counselor. It was a risk that I took for one full year to be successful in landing a job after graduation.

After graduation, I took yet another risk to walk into my purpose, moving away from the great state of Georgia for a job opportunity in Texas. Now I serve as a college counselor at one of the best universities in the state of Texas. I now understand that every decision I've made in the past aligned and created a path for a successful future that I am now living in the present. It's not until the moment when reflecting on your accomplishments that you realize you are able to revel in these achievements because of the time, hard work, and sacrifices you've made. The sacrifices that you make today will lead to some huge successes tomorrow. Always remember that the decisions you make not only change the next moment in time, but they impact your future. Only you can make sacrifices and reap the benefits of them tomorrow. Make sure you choose wisely my friend.

## RQs

What sacrifices have you made that led to successes in your future? How was that moment of realization for you?

# Notes

# **<u>Chapter 8</u>**

## Now

"It's better to live in the present than to be stuck
on yesterday or worried about tomorrow."

Being in the present and focusing your energy on the now
is a moment of balance and serenity. There is something
that you tap into that influences you to be at ease and helps
you to be still. In a life that is fast-paced, chaotic, and most
hectic, being still just for a moment quells the stress and
gives you peace.

Being a future-oriented person who also engages in
self-reflection constantly, I find myself reminiscing on the
past and what I could have done while also assigning
myself tasks to complete for the future. As a thinker, I get
so lost in my own head that sometimes I have to take a step
out, sit, and just breathe. This is when mindfulness steps

in. It is a great tool to use in order to stay grounded and centered in every moment. Being mindful or practicing mindfulness is a critical component when living in the present and enjoying life to the fullest as the old cliché states. I can find myself worried about the next move that I forget to enjoy the current one. I too forget to live in the now.

A college professor and advisor of mine during my graduate work helped me to embrace mindfulness and practice it non-judgmentally. She taught me that it's okay and also normal when practicing mindfulness to have self-defeating thoughts, anxiety, and to be distracted due to some noise nearby. She also taught me to embrace these distractions when they occur and allow them to pass. She helped me understand how the relationship of those small distractions during the mindfulness activities can represent distractions in my everyday life. By embracing them and letting them pass, I did not blame myself for past mistakes or give myself an anxiety attack about future goals. I now challenge you to embrace anxiety, fear, doubt, or other things you wrestle with and to let them pass. Be mindful in every experience, in every moment.

My friend, you cannot time travel to the past or future. You have no control over them and that is okay. The past was. The future will be. The present is all that every really exists. Embrace the now; live in it and accept it. Imagine how much ease and serenity you would feel if only you envelop yourself to this very moment. Your breathing would be steady, and your mind will be still. Forgive yourself for past mistakes. Trust the process of life and enjoy every moment of it, because you only get one.

## RQs

Close your eyes, take a few deep breaths and be still for a minute or two. What does being in the present feel like for you?

# Notes

# **Chapter 9**

## The Small Things

*"No matter what today holds, you're the reason that it's awesome."*
*-Author Unknown*

While working as a resident assistant (RA) in college, I would go to the resident hall's clubhouse in the evenings to work on assignments in the computer lab. One day after a long week of classes, and in all, busyness from the job and everyday stress of being a college student, I felt drained and exhausted. While I was walking out of the computer lab towards the main desk area to speak with my peers, I saw a blue post-it note taped to the table. In my head I made an assumption based on past experiences and thought someone must have left their paper and trash in the lab, and here I go again as an RA that has to pick up trash to keep our hall looking neat and clean.

Finally, I looked down and read the note: "No matter what today holds, you're the reason that it's awesome." I don't know who wrote it and left it there, but I'm glad they did. The message seemed as if it were written specifically for me. To the creator of that blue post-it note message, thank you! After reading it over, I took a picture of it to save as a screensaver. I viewed it many times as I would use my phone. Instead of taking the note, I left it so it could inspire someone else. That small message of hope had a great impact on my day and just about every day after that.

Today, focus on what you have and not on what you don't have. Sometimes we get so caught up in wishing and hoping that things will be better in life that we never appreciate the things that are currently better in the present. No matter how hard life may seem right now or how stretched thin you are, know that you are amazing. Know that you are strong. Also, please know that you're the reason today is awesome. It's the small reminders to ourselves that keep us going and moving ahead in spite of everyday challenges. It's the small things that matter the most.

Read and complete the following. Even though
_____ (insert a problem,
stressor, etc.), I choose to be awesome.

## RQs

What problem or stressor are you currently experiencing?
In spite of the problem or stressor, how will you choose to
be awesome?

# Notes

# __Chapter 10__

## Undefeated

*"Never dim your light for others."*

When you walk into a room, pull your shoulders back, walk with confidence, and hold your head up high. If your presence, talents, or gifts influence someone else to feel insecure, that's because they are making it about them. It has nothing to do with you. Sometimes your light shines so bright that it blinds those around you, and that is okay. Never allow someone to place a shade on your light because *their* light needs to be brightened.

Whether you are in a class setting or work environment, someone will always have something negative to say about you in order to distract you from succeeding. They may spread rumors about you or throw dirt on your name. As the rose does, you will have to grow through the dirt in order to blossom into your fullest potential. Never feel less than or portray yourself as if you are, because my friend, you are not. You are talented. You are gifted. You are undefeated. You cannot afford to jeopardize your purpose or call for others. Sometimes holding on to modesty can cost you your destiny. Be grateful for the obstacles, failures, and naysayers, for they will fuel your endurance to rise above.

They may twist you and bend you, but never let them break you. They may distract you and attack you, but never let them see you sweat. You have been gifted with the proper tools not to overcome the pressure, to fend off the attacks, and to break free from the chains that are the tongues of enemies. Don't make a letdown into a knockout. Every "no" is not forever. Not every applause is a helping hand. Know the difference by having discernment, by having that keen eye that can see beyond the facades of plastic smiles and limp handshakes.

Forgive those who have persecuted you for having a bright light. Not in order to forget, but to have a piece of mind in order to fully attract future opportunities and blessings. Your light will be your guide to a brighter future. Your undefeated spirit will create room for your success, and your talents will be a foundation to create other opportunities for those who come after you.

Remember to always walk in grace, embrace humility, and be undefeated.

## RQs

Think about a time someone tried to dim your light. How did it feel? How did you react?

# Notes

# **Chapter 11**

## Adjusting

*"Discomfort builds resilience."*

Periods of adjustment take time and great effort. Adjusting to a new place or situation is never easy. Just when you thought you had the tools and skills needed to sift through a period of adjustment, you learn that some of those skills are outdated and need to be replaced with some new, up-to-date tools. Whether you are starting a new job, graduating college, or moving across the country, adjusting is not always easy. In that period of adjustment, you can sometimes find yourself alone with no support, no guidance, and no one to turn to. For me, adjusting to life after college was very much debilitating. I moved to Texas to start my career as a college counselor and it felt as if my whole support system caved right under me. The people who I depended on before were not there when I needed them the most.

I was in a period of involuntary isolation. But this was the perfect opportunity to grow in my career and in life on a whole. When I reflect on my first couple of months here in Texas, they were uncomfortable. Being here on my own brought about some cold and lonely nights. There were days where tears would fall without warning. There were nights when I couldn't sleep. I had to dig deep inside myself to find some inspiration, some hope. I had to sit and experience my discomfort. I could not run from, nor could I push it away. I had to dig deep and find my resilience. I had to understand that my story and my experience was a reminder that when things are cloudy and tough, the sun will soon shine again. Each day I reminded myself, "Today is a new day. Take a breath and keep moving forward."

If you are in a period of adjustment, remember that without discomfort, resilience will surely not grow. Life sometimes takes you out of your comfort zone and forces you to acquire new tools and skills that you will be necessary in the next chapter in your life. You are where you need to be, my friend. If you were able to land an interview and got accepted, you belong there. Don't let fear, doubt, or insecurities run you away from your blessing place. You have the tools needed to be there and will learn some new tools along the way. With opposition comes opportunities, in resistance there is resiliency, and cloudy moments bring clarity. Some days may feel long, and some nights may be dark. You may experience some grief and also some loss. Your elevation in your education, career, and in life will take you to a place where you have to give up what is comfortable and what is familiar for something unknown. The discomfort that you are feeling is helping you to be consistent, not complacent. To accept complacency is to abort your dream, purpose, or potential. This period of adjustment is pushing you to be one step closer to your purpose and destiny.

Having an inborn drive and a spirit of determination can help you navigate through your period of adjustment. Believing that you belong and that you are enough are mantras to help see you through that tough time. Be consistent, not complacent. Continue to learn, grow, and have hope.

## RQs

What period of adjustment are you currently in? What tools or skills can you use to ease your discomfort?

# Notes

# Chapter 12

## Reflection

*"New experiences bring new perspectives."*

Self-reflection helps me grow and helps me remember when I succeeded. It gives me some insight into my own behaviors and patterns. It influences me to be intentional about my life and what I expect out of it. It gives me a new perspective and vision to foresee my future. It allows me to dig a little deeper and reach for compassion, gratitude, and forgiveness; traits necessary for personal growth. Giving yourself compassion in reflection feeds your worth and self-esteem. Gratitude in reflection feeds your spirit in order to help yourself be thankful for past experiences when you have fallen short of personal expectations. Forgiveness and mercy are pieces needed to understand that even though you were tough on yourself or engaged in self-sabotaging and negative self-talk, you can give yourself a second chance to start over and learn from past mistakes.

Reflection is a moment to observe, reminisce, and meditate on past experiences. It's a moment to evaluate the positive things that went well and also to uncover some challenges encountered. Reflection is a necessary task to engage in when moving to another level in life. It provides you the space to understand your old habits and patterns that have been subconsciously woven into your behaviors and attitudes. It teaches you how to disrupt those patterns and create a new narrative moving forward. Reflection exposes your weaknesses and strengths; your achievements and areas of growth. In reflection, you learn what to let go of. Reflection exposes lies we tell ourselves about our life experiences. It reveals what we deny, hold onto, or cover up. If you want to know the truth about yourself, take a look in the mirror because it never lies. Reflection exposes the truth. It makes visible what was, is, and is to come. It helps us learn from previous experiences and life situations. It helps us shape a new perspective and provides the space to reevaluate what we need, want, and hope to achieve. It's essential to help us move beyond past emotional pain, mistakes, and could haves.

My friend, reflection is a key component in life to continue moving forward. Reflection helps keep you motivated to strive for excellence and to help give you strength to carry on just a little further. When you self-reflect and stare at your behaviors, thoughts, and actions, it gives you a sense of clarity about how and why you do the things you do. It allows you to see yourself a little deeper, to clean and strengthen your inner self in order to produce works beneficial and encouraging to others.

## RQs

When was the last time you participated in self-reflection? What did you learn about yourself?

# Notes

# **Chapter 13**

## Grace

*"Your expectations won't always be met—and that's okay."*

Expectations are what we use in order to hold some experience or person to a standard. What is funny about expectations is that they only come from the person creating them and not the person(s) held to these standards. I believe that we get hurt or feel rejected when people don't meet our expectations because we haven't actually shared said expectations. What we do is make assumptions as to what someone else will do, and then become disappointed when our unvoiced expectation is left hanging. After feeling rejected, letdown, and unheard so many times, I reflected on what information I was not relaying in those situations. I've come to learn that I created narratives in my head such as "people didn't care," "my voice was silenced," or "I didn't matter." It wasn't that others disregarded my needs or desires, it was that I didn't communicate what I expected out of a group assignment, relationship, or experience.

Now, I live life with a small disclaimer that if people or things don't meet my expectations, it is okay. Because if I don't share what I expect, how am I supposed to hold someone accountable for them? This can also be viewed from another perspective. When you do share your expectations and people fall short of it, forgive them anyway. Maybe they didn't have the proper tools or skills to meet them in the first place. Just remember to embrace and express grace always because I'm sure there were times before where you fell short of meeting someone else's expectations whether intentionally or unintentionally.

## RQs

When was a time your expectations weren't met? Did you share them with others, or did you just assume they would understand?

# Notes

# <u>Chapter 14</u>

## Potential

*"It's an amazing feeling when God allows you to tap into your potential."*

As a counselor and even as a human being, I believe that everyone has the potential within themselves to overcome any obstacle or issue they face in life. I believe that the potential or the solutions to their problem comes from within. The barrier to unleashing that potential is that some people are afraid of what they may find or have internalized negative beliefs about themselves in their given situation. When a person allows themselves to engage in self-criticism, self-sabotage, and self-doubt, they create a wall that becomes almost impenetrable. This wall also serves to limit their potential, because it gives them room to make excuses if they don't achieve a goal or use their gifts appropriately. It serves to lower their expectations of themselves, and this in turns lowers their standards. But even these individuals can still push themselves (or become inspired) to realize their potentials. When they tap into their potential and get a taste of what that is like, they can be unstoppable.

Everyone is born with unique abilities, gifts, and talents. Many people are born with a set purpose in life. It is the responsibility of that person to learn about their gifts, nurture them, and utilize them to uplift themselves and others around them. When you tap into your potential and feel its power, the only person that can stop you from unleashing it and using it to its fullest impact is yourself. Get out of your own way!

When you cultivate or nurture your gifts and talents, you continue to grow. You build upon the foundational gifts you have and learn different ways to share them and to inspire others. Most of the time when you walk into a room, you will not need to say anything because your gifts and talents will make enough noise for you. They will create space for you even when there doesn't seem to be enough room for you to fit. They will help mold and shape you in a perfect way to fit with all the other puzzles pieces (people) of your job, business, life, etc.

Don't ignore the call when your purpose finds you. Ignoring the call extends the time in which you live life with only a fraction of the power that is within you. Potential is an innate aspect of yourself that only you are able to tap into. Whatever ideas or thoughts you have; create, reflect, explore it, and know that the idea was given to you for a reason. Tap into your potential and learn to unleash it. You never know all of what you have until you tap into it and explore it.

## RQs

Have you tapped into your potential? If so, how did it feel? If not, what's stopping you?

# Notes

# **Chapter 15**

## The Journey

*"Enjoy your journey to the top." -Amber Mann*

Friends truly do come, and they surely do go. Many people are sent into our lives for a chapter in time, while a few stays for the entire book. When you have a friend that wholeheartedly has your back and best interest at heart, never let them go. Miss no opportunity to show them your appreciation; send them random text messages and emails, always express gratitude, and remember to always be their biggest supporter too. I have many close friends who have inspired and supported me through so many trials and obstacles life has thrown my way. One in particular that I can think of that has been consistent and genuine is my good friend, Amber Mann. We met in college working for a department on our campus one summer. We had mutual friends on the same staff, so we had heard things about each other, but we had never met in person. In fact, that was the first thing she said to me, "Hi, I'm Amber, and I've heard a lot about you." I replied with a matching response. From the first conversation and many others after that, we formed a close and deep connection.

Amber graduated college before I did, so months had passed before we got the chance to see each other again. We always wanted to visit each other, but plans had a way of falling through over and over again. There never seemed to be a good time to meet and catch up until one weekend, while on a trip with some frat brothers, I invited her to lunch with us. While catching up over lunch with my good friend, we shared our future goals, hopes, and aspirations with each other.

While sharing my calling and aspiration to write, we both discussed how we could envision life after we finally became successful. I shared that I wanted to wake up the next day and for it to already have happened. Amber questioned my intent in rushing to be successful and told me to enjoy my journey to the top. The manner in which she delivered that short phrase held a lot of weight at that moment. I told her, "Thank you." I expressed how I appreciated her for always keeping me in check and reminding me to pace myself. I joked and said, "Once I start my book, I'm putting that as a quote in it." She laughed dismissively, yet here it is at the beginning of this chapter. To my good friend Amber, I dedicate this chapter to you. Thank you for your support, time spent in person and on the phone listening to me. Continue to do great things in your field of hospitality. Continue to be an inspiration for others.

Enjoying the journey to the top reminds me to pace myself of course and it also reminds me to learn in every moment. It reminds me to see the bigger picture and motivates me to persevere through any hardship I face. It reminds me that success isn't easy to achieve, and that life is about taking things slow; taking one step at a time. Enjoying the journey reminds me to pause, breathe, reflect, and to continue moving forward. It influences me to keep my eyes on the vision and purpose of my life. When storms come and there is trouble all around me, it whispers to keep pressing on. It reminds me that my life is not my own and that my purpose is much bigger than I can imagine.

No matter what goal or vision you set for yourself, remember to enjoy the journey. You will get there eventually. Remember to pace yourself, reflect, and learn from your mistakes. The journey is not a sprint, it is a marathon.

## RQs

What journey are you currently experiencing? Who or what keeps you motivated?

# Notes

# Chapter 16

## Forward Movement

*"Today, focus on your GREATNESS and not
your limitations."*

Every so often when a person is ready to go to the next
level in life, they look around and remind themselves of
everything they don't have instead of zoning in on what
they *do* have. They tend to forget that everything they have
is all that is needed, and the things they expect to have or
want is extra baggage that cannot be placed on the flight to
their next destination. Focusing on your greatness helps
you curb your doubts, low self-esteem, and negative
beliefs. It shines a light on your strengths, success, and
achievements. It propels you forward once you let go and

externalize your belief of not being equipped, strong, worthy, or good enough.

Many people become stuck in stages of life when they feel that a waking moment will not look any better, because of their belief about themselves or belief about their current situation. The mind is oh so powerful! We have been programmed and socialized to conform and live our lives up to the expectations and desires of others. We focus on the things others have and create the narrative that we need the things they have to look or feel better about ourselves. We compare instead of conquer. The belief and doubts that bombard us daily limits the talents and gifts that can be used to walk fully in our purpose on earth. When we create limiting beliefs and narratives about our lives, we limit ourselves on what we can become.

Forward movement is about not looking back. Forward movement is about pushing yourself a little harder. It's about staying up a little longer to read about how to jumpstart your business, putting in more time to master your craft, and about limiting distractions to live in your purpose. It is time to get moving, my friend. Move towards your goal and don't look back. Once you reach that level, remember not to take backward steps. It's easy to fall prey to those terrible twins, doubt and fear. It is also easy to hold yourself back. Moving forward requires energy. It requires you to practice motivating yourself and affirming that you have all that is needed to reach the next phase or level in life. It's about being appreciative that even though life may throw tomatoes at you, you can pick them up and throw them back. It's about taking ownership of your destiny and loving every minute of it by giving it all that you got.

## RQs

What greatness are you holding back? What is limiting you from unleashing it?

# Notes

# **Chapter 17**

## Self-Care

*"Give from your overflow, not from your cup."*

When people ask me for my definition of self-care, I almost always respond with, "saying no." Saying no, setting boundaries, and doing things that bring me peace continue to and will always create the space for me to pour back into myself. Without first pouring into myself, for how long will I be able to pour into others? What I share with friends, relatives, and clients is that you cannot give from an empty vessel. If your cup is dry, then it is time to fill it back up. What I learned from my own personal counselor is that if you don't have it to give, then don't. If you do have it to give and the intention is to give, simply do just that. You decide on how much and how often others can take from you. If your energy and power are depleted and you continue to give without stopping, you are unclear about your limitations and unclear about your boundaries.

As a recovering people-pleaser, I had to let go of the "If I say no, they may not like me" mentality. Being the "strong one," "the one who has it together," and the "one who always says yes" has gotten me into trouble so many times. Naturally, I am a giver as a friend, son, mentor, and counselor. I am not saying giving or helping others is a bad thing, yet what I am saying is that it can leave you feeling empty and drained if done more than often. Engaging in self-care is not a selfish act. It is an act of filling yourself up of what's needed and then some, to pour back into others.

When I engage in self-care, I usually pray, journal/write down my thoughts, meditate, relax, exercise, or binge-watch a Netflix series. In this time, I spend time with myself to give my body, mind, and soul a well-needed break. One thing for sure, I try to be intentional about setting boundaries. Setting boundaries teaches you a lot about yourself, and a lot about others.

Boundaries allow you to set limits on how much you give. Boundaries allow you to take a break. They allow you to communicate how much you are willing, able, or simply not going to do. They allow you to say I can do this, yet I won't do that. They also give you autonomy and independence to just say no. When you set boundaries, those who support and love you dearly will understand and those who don't may become angry or bitter. Either way, understand that boundaries are needed when you have a calling and need to take a break to refill your cup to continue your work in walking in your purpose. Giving from a full cup requires less energy and giving from an empty one is exhausting. Remember: Give from your saucer, not your cup.

## RQs

How do you participate in self-care? How do you refill your cup?

# Notes

# __Chapter 18__

## The Work

This book is a collection of my thoughts, experiences, and a bit of inspiration. I am no expert or specialist when it comes to finding your purpose or calling. However, I am a witness to how self-reflection, self-compassion, and believing you are enough can change your life.

By now, I hope you have gained some awareness about what your purpose here on earth is. I hope that this book has given you some motivation to act on your ideas, and even the inspiration to tap into your inner potential to become who you were destined to be. I pray that you are more in tune with yourself, have reflected on your experiences and learned some new life lessons throughout the reading. Maybe you know what you're called to do. Maybe you don't. Either way, it's up to you to do the work to figure it out. As of now, I will continue to do my work and hope that it is meaningful. I want my work here on earth to be inspiring, thought-provoking, and authentic. What about you?

# Acknowledgements

I want to give thanks to God my heavenly father, counselor, and creator. You've given me so many gifts and talents. I work tenaciously just to hear you say, "well done."

**Warren Taye & Stephanie Wright:** You both are amazing parents! Thank you for your loving-kindness, and for modeling the art of hard work and dedication.

**Devin:** Thank you for being one of my biggest supporters and laughing confidante. I'm proud of you little brother.

**Eddie:** Thanks for creating my book cover design and for also serving as a consultant in this process. Your support will never go unnoticed.

Owner and CEO
Edspression Designs, LLC
edpressions@gmail.com

**Nehemiah, Jessica, Chandler, Shane, and Shawn:** Thank you for looking to me for advice and keeping me on my toes as a mentor.

**Shun:** Thank you for always saying a prayer for me and being a messenger of God.

**Jasmine and Jada:** Thank you for assisting me in this process and for proofreading my drafts.

**Adam:** Thanks for being my editor. With your help, my message has been amplified.

**TreVoy Kelly:** Thank you for all of my amazing pictures.
TreVoy Kelly Photography
Info@treyvoykellyphotography.com

A big, "Thank you!" to everyone else who have supported me in the process of writing this book. Without your guidance and support, this book would have not been completed.

# About the Author

Warren B. Wright, M.Ed., LPC-Intern, NCC is a native of South Carolina who traveled around the world as a military child. While attending college, Warren embarked on a journey of self-discovery. On this journey, he learned about his purpose, inner potential, and worth through the art of self-reflection. In this book, he challenges you to do the same. He shares about life lessons with the use of quotes and gives nuggets of wisdom. Whether you've experienced pain, isolation, or doubt, this book will help you find meaning, dispel self-negative beliefs, and will motivate you.

Warren is an alumnus of Georgia Southern University where he completed his undergraduate and graduate studies, making him a Double Eagle. He now resides in Bryan/College Station, TX where he serves as a counselor for the Student Counseling Service Division of Student Affairs at Texas A&M University. In this role, he conducts individual and group counseling using an integrative multicultural-constructivist approach, to motivate his clients to change their narratives about themselves and their situation. As an author, presenter, and speaker, Warren fosters a sense of authenticity, worthiness (You are enough), and hope.

# <u>Contact Warren</u>

Contact me via email for speaking engagements, panel discussions, Q&A, etc.

**Email:** contactwarrenwright@gmail.com

**Instagram:** _warrenbrandon

**Twitter:** WarrenBWright

**Facebook:** Warren Brandon

Made in the USA
Columbia, SC
02 May 2019